Goog

Adwords For

Beginners:

Learn How to Advertise, Market Products and Services Effectively Using Google Adwords Ads

By

Dale Blake

Table of Contents

Introduction 5

Chapter 1. How to Create an Effective Ad in Google AdWords For a Product or Service 7

Chapter 2. Price-Per-Click Considerations on Google AdWords 13

Chapter 3. Conversion Expectations 17

Chapter 4. Estimated Ad Budget Requirements 19

Chapter 5. Using Bid Simulators 21

Chapter 6. Using The Bid Simulator with Shopping Campaigns 23

Chapter 7. Things to Keep in Mind While Using Bid Simulators 27

Conclusion 28

Thank You Page 30

Google Adwords For Beginners: Learn How to Advertise, Market Products and Services Effectively Using Google Adwords Ads

By Dale Blake

Introduction

Imagine a situation where you could advertise your business in a newspaper or magazine and only pay a small amount of money when someone reads your advert. It does not happen in magazines but that is the concept behind Pay-Per-Click in online adverts. Pay-Per-Click is a term that refers to advertising, whereby the advertiser will only pay for their advert when a user clicks on it, rather than just viewing it. Just like any other advertising method, Google AdWords can be optimized to bring more targeted traffic to your website. Methods of optimization range from creating beautiful ads with catchy phrases to keyword optimization. You have to beware of the location of your business as well as your region of interest.

Advertisers do not have to pay anything in order to create their adverts with Google AdWords. The process is totally free and you can make as any ads as you need. Since it is an automated program, AdWords will place your adverts on Google every time a user searches for a specific set of keywords. This is ideal since your ad will reach many people, who are interested in similar products. As a Pay-Per-Click advertising program, the views that your advert accumulates will not be charged. It is advantageous to corporates and individuals alike since it makes it a very budget friendly way of advertising. Additionally, a view means that users may have read your advert so they may visit your site later. AdWords brings targeted visitors to your website. As long as you have created the advert, chosen targeted keywords, selected an appropriate budget, your ad is ready to be displayed and viewed thousands of times. Your funds will only be deducted when someone clicks on the advert. The views are free.

Chapter 1. How to Create an Effective Ad in Google AdWords For a Product or Service

Advertisements are the best way to make your products and services known to the general public. For this reason, it is vital that you make the best out of them to gain popularity even to those customers who were initially not aware of the existence of the particular products and services in question. Advancements in technology have enabled product and service owners advertise their products through the internet.

Google AdWords is currently the best place to make such advertisements. It works best when someone is in the research mode. The moment you search for a keyword, the Google gives a variety of options, most of which are advertisements. He following guidelines may make an advertisement effective to the public especially when using Google AdWords to make you search.

An effective advert knows best what consumers demand for. If consumers are not searching for your product and/or services in Google then be sure that advertising on AdWords is not the right place to do so. Targeting the right audience for your advert is also an important consideration to make. Make sure that you set the right language and countries in which you would want to make your sales volume large. Majority of the population should speak the language in which you opt to make your advertisement in.

It is obvious that if you decide to make your advert on Google AdWords you will not be the only product and service owner who will be advertising their products on the same website. There will be many other more competitors with the same products and services like the ones you are offering. For this reason you need to stay on the top of the game and overshadow your competitors. This you can do by looking at what other successful sellers have done in the past and collecting, organizing and utilizing such information much better than they did.

Make your advert irresistible to read, for customers to request for more information and most of all for them to make their purchases. For an offer to be irresistible, it ought to have be valuable, believable, and able to reduce risk oriented actions and ultimately call for consumer action.

The products and service in which you advertise in the internet need to be valuable. This means that its value has to above the price tag for which it is put for sale. Caution however should be taken so as not to mistake the products and services for being cheap. All you need to do is clearly make known to your consumers the worth of value such goods and services will offer them regardless of the price tag.

Consumers are the worst people to lie to. They always need and want to be told the truth and explained to why product and service offers may be lower than those of other advertisers by a great deal. For an advert to be effective, it also need to be believable. Consumers may become skeptical in buying very cheap goods and services because they may assume it is faulty in some way or the other. For an effective advert to push through you need to outline if it holds special reasons such as clearing of inventory, end-of-year-sale, celebration of an anniversary, opening a new store and so on.

One major secret to creating an effective advert on Google AdWord is creating one that calls for action through the KISS method. This means you need to Keep It Simple and Stupid. Simplicity will draw consumers to take action by making purchases and orders. Stupidity on the other hand is not literal. It means advertisers should be flexible and play around with consumer psychology. This they can do by making a steep reduction in their discount rates but seeking to benefit from another totally different section like that after-sale services like servicing.

No single person would allow themselves to get robbed through the internet. Once you establish an advertisement you also need to give your consumers back up plan to make their money deposits in case they decide to take a step in making purchases and ordering for your goods. A money back guarantee is one way to assure your consumers of excellent service delivery failure to which their money will be returned in full amounts. This is one great way to stay ahead of your competitors as consumers will always feel safe with a seller who guarantees their money safety.

Use very captivation keywords in your advert. The moment consumers begin to click and search for your products and services that is the moment you too need to adjust your bids accordingly. If you are earning good profit margins go ahead and raise your bids but if this is not the case then you need to think twice and lower your bids.

The type of words you use in your advert will determine whether consumers will be interested to read more or not. Begin your advert with a word that is captivating and grabs consumer attention. Use such magic words as "free", "new", "offer" among others. Other such like word that that provoke consumer emotion, enthusiasm and response include cheap, tips, discover, fact, at last, free shipping, sale, special offer, time limited offer, tricks, etc.

Other phrases may invite consumers to take an action in ordering and requesting for services. Depending on the business you intend to promote, make sure the phrases are tailor made to the specific products and services in question or else Google may fail to acknowledge it at all. Examples include 'buy today and save up to 50%', 'download free trial now', 'sales end tomorrow' etc.

Google is here to stay, and so is Google AdWords. Advertisements are an always-continuing series of tests that product and service owners need to change frequently according to what consumers are in the look for. Advertisers need to keep track of their adverts and read through consumer's questions so that their concerns are answered.

Chapter 2. Price-Per-Click Considerations on Google AdWords

Price per click, is also known as cost-per-click (CPC). You can set the highest possible price on the cost of someone by the virtue of them just clicking at your AdWord advert. You are able to settle and acquire the most out of this bidding method because you only get to make payments when a viewer gains much interest to the point of clicking your ad. In this bidding method, you are required to set a maximum cost-per click bid which simply implies that it is the highest amount that you will be required to pay for in case of a click on your ad.

An example is given that of you think the value of having someone visit your website is 30 cents, then this is the amount that you can set as your maximum. You will be required to pay that maximum amount if in any case a person reads your ad and goes ahead to click it. Alternatively, you will not be required to part with any amounts if no one clicks it.

Price-per-click type of bidding gives users the following two options. One, the manual bidding where you get to enjoy and have the opportunity to choose your own amounts for the bid. Two, the automatic bidding where it is the sole responsibility of the AdWords to set your maximum bid amounts. This will be set according to your overall budget.

It is usually your maximum bid amount that you will be charged but sometimes it may be much less than expected. The rank of your Ad to a great extent determines the position of your ad on various search results in the search network in question. This particular rank is a score that one gets to earn based on the maximum set amounts. Your maximum will only stand a chance to increase depending on your price-per-click bid and the quality of your ad as compared to that of other similar advertisers.

It is possible to choose your most favorable bidding strategy depending on your goals. Every single time a person does their search on Google, AdWords performs an action to determine the ads that appear on the result page and their positional rank on the page. Before you place your ad in this auction method, you need to choose how to make your bid in advance. Your bidding options will be made to depend on various optional reasons like for getting impressions, clicks or even conversions.

When you focus on impressions, the bidding method is recognized as cost-per-impressions or CPM bid. This is one method that is highly recommended if increasing the awareness of your brand is your main goal. Those that focus on conversions take specific action on your website soon after clicking on one of your ads. Cost-per-acquisition also CPA bid on the other hand is recommended for AdWords that are seasonal and for those who are interested in conversions like signups and making of purchases.

One is capable of applying maximum bids in so many ways. You in any case you require all the keywords in an ad to possess similar bids, all you need is to set an ad group as a default bid. If you make two dollars to appear as your Cost-per-click then that will represent your maximum. The most recent and easiest way to take control of your cost-per-click is to have all your keywords filtered when one is searched online.

Another way to maximize on your bids is to set different cost-per-click for the different items on the keyword search network. If your desire is to have different bids, you are required to set keyword bids independently from each other. First n of all, you need to study your consumers and note the kind of item that has most clicks. For that which is mostly searched, you might decide to raise the maximum bid by a given amount. For example if you deal in electronic ads, you notice laptops are mostly searched on by many compared to iPads. To raise your cost-per-click, you opt to raise that of laptops to read at 40 cents per click and maintain that of iPads at 30 cents per click. This way you still have the opportunity to maintain your ads and keep up the pace with other competitors.

Chapter 3. Conversion Expectations

Google conversion rates are directly related to the conversion rates. Even though very few people who are advertising take the time to think of their click through expectations, understanding how much to expect from each AdWord served will help you gauge the success of your campaign.

The success of your AdWords campaign will depend on the type of advertising you settle for. If you would rather work with impressions, you have accept the fact that your adverts will be dished out to views regardless of whether the visitors click or not. This makes this type of AdWords not appropriate to people who are interested in traffic that translates back to their own websites.

To people who are just out to present the message, and nothing else, impression adverts are a sufficient alternative. You will not have to pay a fortune for them as you would have with pay per click adverts and you will still get an ample share of the audience. However, if you are interested in visitors getting back to your site, you have to invest in the click adverts.

If you decide to work with click adverts, you will always get the right click through since you will always get the real value of each click. This means that you can safely put your conversion to 100 percent. However, the only thing that you will not have control over is what the clicks registered do once they get to your landing page. They might leave, peruse and leave, or make a purchase. This, therefore, will alter what the true definition of conversion is. If you measure conversion by people getting to your website, then this is a 100 percent conversion. If you add more value to this, then the conversion rate will definitely vary.

Chapter 4. Estimated Ad Budget Requirements

When it zeroes down to cost estimates for your AdWords campaign, there is more to work on than you previously imagined. Your budget requirements depend on a couple of factors ranging from the click volume estimates to the competitiveness of the industry.

You need to develop a rule about the lowest threshold for your company as far as the number of daily click the campaign should capture is concerned. For corporates and big business, a minimum of 10-20 per day is okay. Anything less than that will not count much since converting a click into a client is actually another complex process that entails customizing your website. There is usually the need to capture more traffic whenever you think of posting an ad. However, with a campaign like AdWords, the quality of the click should always come first at any given point. If you are determined to have your campaign collect an average of 10 clicks in a day, the simple calculation below will help you estimate how much you will spend on the campaign.

If you chose a group of keywords and a target market that has an average Cost Per Click of $3, you will need at least $3x10=$30 in a day to get 10 clicks. This does not mean that the average Cost Per Click for most adverts is $3, in fact, many of the less competitive keywords and products range between $0.15-$0.8. This will greatly influence the budget that you will spend.

In your bid to place an advert, you will note that each industry has its own standard of conversion and the minimum budget that you need in order to compete with the already established brands may vary greatly. Industries like banking and insurance tend to have a higher click through ratio than those dealing with foodstuffs and cosmetics.

Chapter 5. Using Bid Simulators

Sometimes doing all the mathematics on each keyword is cumbersome and you need an automated process to make the calculations and determine which one suits you best. Regular bid simulators will give you an insight into how your ad will perform in a week and the max CPC bid you should expect to spend. It is integrated in to the ad group and keyword tab of Google AdWords, and is simple to use. The shopping bid simulator will let you estimate how given changes on your bid would impact the impression, clicks and cost of your campaign. This useful but simple tool is found on the products group tab. Another important simulator is the campaign bid simulator, which is used to model and apply changes on your bid across the campaign level. It is found on the campaigns tab.

The three simulators come in handy in multiple instances when you are using Google AdWords. For example, if you have an approximate budget of between US$120-150 and you would like to place adverts with a maximum CPC bid of US$0.91 for your keyword, the bid simulator will help you see estimates of the clicks, impressions, cost, conversions and the conversion value to expect with every value of the approximate budget. You will therefore choose an appropriate budget that has good value for money. In case the budget is not enough for the campaign, the simulators will indicate the same and advise you on the appropriate budget that would generate the desired results.

Chapter 6. Using The Bid Simulator with Shopping Campaigns

Concerning shopping campaigns, the bid simulator actually collects and analyses relevant data from Google ad auctions that have been active in the previous 7 days while using your competitor's bids, product data and quality of your ads as measures to get accurate results. The simulator then uses this acquired information to make an estimate of how a given change or changes to the bid would affect its cost, impressions and clicks. You can use the simulator to gauge the performance of an individual product, a group of products with categories or even a plain collection of products.

If you are using the bid simulator for a given group of products with subdivisions, you have an option to view the bid changes in aggregate and even model the changes for the non-excluded product groups. This is effective even in instances where the data on a given product group is not enough.

Bid scaling is useful in predicting the changes that you are to expect if you decreased or increased the bids of a given product group by a percentage of your choice. In just a few clicks, you can apply the changes to any given number of products. The only place where you will not use bid scaling is if the product groups are subdivided by an item id. In the event that you want to change the bids in a given product group into a fixed value' or apply a change to all the products within certain groups, the bid simulator will make it easier for you. In this instance, your default group bids will change to the fixed value and the product group-level bids removed.

If you have a limited budget, bid changes across multiple product groups will help you reach many people since they increase traffic significantly. The bid simulator will show you the projected costs for bid changes and whether you might need to adjust your current budget to meet the most appropriate bid that has the most significant returns.

The bid simulator will help you get the estimates of the expenditures even in complex situations. For example, suppose you are to place a US$0.8 bid on a product group, say 'Travel Companies' and you are curious at the moment to know the results that you will get when you place a bid of US$1.5 or even US$2.5, the simulator will provide an estimate of the number of clicks you will get. Additionally, it shows the costs and the impressions that you would have seen with the other bids that you are curious to find out about.

You can also get estimates of the budget you are to spend should you opt for placing bids on two product groups within a same subdivision. For instance, if 'Travel Companies' is a subdivision and 'Europe Tours' and 'Asia Tours' are groups within the subdivision, and the later has a bid of US$1 while the former has US$2, you can use the bid scaling option to see the potential impact of any changes in the percentage of the product groups within the subdivision. If you try increasing the bid by 10%, 'Europe Tours' will have a bid of US$1.10 and 'Asia Tours' will have a bid of US$2.2. You are therefore able to see the estimates to expect in case you increase your bid by any given percentage.

If you choose to use the product group-wide option, you will be in a position to see the effect of setting a bid across two product groups in the same subdivision.

You just have to select this option, enter your bid and you will see the estimates of the results to expect.

The bid simulator not only shows what to expect when you place an ad. You can also use it to see how your bids could have affected the performance of the ads over the last week. Although you may see how some bids can perform, it does not provide accurate results due to factors beyond its scope. First, the volume of searches is bound to change from one day to the next and the number of adverts vying for similar keywords might increase causing competition to be stiffer.

Chapter 7. Things to Keep in Mind While Using Bid Simulators

You will not be able to use the bid simulator if you set your products to 'excluded' or if your products are using an Item ID attribute. These settings are easy to change –you can do it whenever necessary. The data that is displayed on the simulators is based on the traffic that you received in the past 7 days. Therefore, if there are any changes in the trends or you changed your bid, there may be a difference between the actual data and the projections given by the bid simulator.

If you are not seeing the simulator for a product group when on Product Listing Ads, it means that the data accrued about them may not be enough to give an estimate. The only way to counter this is by letting the ads run for a little longer. Afterwards, you will have enough reason to use the simulator to determine how the advertisement will perform or have performed within the period they have been in action. If you have placed the products but you are not seeing the tool, you would need to improve the product data or revise the bid for that particular product group.

Conclusion

Taking the above-mentioned points in to consideration, AdWords is an unrivalled genius in the advertising sector. However, do not wrongly interpret the accolades it accrues to mean that it works perfectly with everything. Failure and losses are part of the equation too. Before you embark on any campaign, consider a couple of facts including the services and products you offer, age group that you would like to reach, the kind of websites the advert is supposed to display and keywords you are targeting.

You have complete influence on your budget –you can pause the adverts when you need and resume at your own discretion. Likewise, you can opt for setting a budget that you would like to spend on a given period and you will not be charged a cent more. In terms of value for money, AdWords ranks high since you are only required to pay for clicks on your adverts rather than views as it is with many other advertising networks. Additionally, there are detailed reports indicating the performance of your adverts, which means that you can see the keywords that perform best, age group of your customers and regions that generate more leads to your site. It is simple to get started, easy to stop or pause and most of all, worth your money.

Thank You Page

I want to personally thank you for reading my book. I hope you found information in this book useful and I would be very grateful if you could leave your honest review about this book. I certainly want to thank you in advance for doing this.

If you have the time, you can check my other books too.

Lightning Source UK Ltd.
Milton Keynes UK
UKHW021818270219
338151UK00014B/270/P